新修訂 ◆ 中英對照
ised Edition with Bilingual Reading

山海天人

Mountain, Ocean,
Sky and People :
A Mind Journey through the Dharma Realm

心‧遊‧法‧界

U0056727

心道法師────著
By Dharma Master Hsin Tao

心遊法界金剛歌

南無咕嚕貝

禮敬本初普賢王　大悲遍主觀自在
三身總集蓮華生　加持自顯金剛歌

此心即是大法界　一切眾生即法界
一切諸佛即法界　此即自性法界理

若欲趣入於法界　差別相中入無別
無差別中差別入　一切處中即法界
無所入中入法界　於此四句能趣入
一心法界由此顯　此即趣入之要訣

若欲安住於法界　住一切處而無住
離一切相住無生　行住坐臥與言談
當下安住亦無住　此即安住之要訣

若欲相應於法界　發起慈悲菩提心
廣行一切六度行　自覺覺他覺行圓
生活當下義殊意　悲心周遍普賢行
海印三昧佛心定　周遍含容法界性

Vajra Song on A Mind Journey through the Dharma Realm

Namo Guru Bei!

Homage to the primordial Vairocana King Buddha
The great compassionate Guan Yin Bodhisattva
The unification of three bodies of Guru Rinpoche
Blessed by this self manifesting vajra song

This mind is the great Dharma realm
All sentient beings are the Dharma realm
All Buddhas are the Dharma realm
This is the truth of the self nature of the Dharma realm

If one wants to enter the Dharma realm
Enter non-discrimination through discriminated forms
Enter discrimination through non-discriminated forms
Everywhere is the Dharma realm
Enter the Dharma realm through entering nowhere
If one can understand these four sentences
The Dharma realm of one mind manifests from here
This is the key to understanding

If one wants to abide in the Dharma realm
Abide everywhere and nowhere
Abandon every form and abide in non-arising
Walking, living, sitting, lying down and speaking
Abide in the present moment and non-abiding
This is the key to true abiding

If one wants to respond in the Dharma realm
Develop the compassionate bodhicitta
Completely practice the six perfections
Awaken yourself and others and perfect the action of awakening
Follow the wisdom of Manjushri Bodhisattva in the present moment of life
Follow the universal compassionate action of Vairocana Bodhisattva
The Samadhi of the ocean seal is the Samadhi of Buddha's mind
The nature of the Dharma realm is universal and all-embracing

本書以山海天人之概念，彰顯華嚴的四法界觀。山對應於事法界，海對應於理事無礙法界，天對應於理法界，人對應於事事無礙法界。其對應之理，如偈所云：

山：華嚴聖山入法界　　事法界中說俗諦
海：毘盧性海歸體性　　理事無礙心即佛
天：虛空法身無言說　　理法界中體性空
人：普賢行願窮三際　　事事無礙菩薩行

山之章
華嚴聖山入法界　事法界中說俗諦

華嚴聖山入法界

山之章的主要意象，就是靈鷲山，此處所顯的靈鷲山，即無盡莊嚴的華嚴聖山。本章希望一切眾生，都能經由靈鷲山傳承的引導，而進入法界之中。

事法界中說俗諦

本章的主旨是「說俗諦」，所謂的俗諦，乃是隨順世俗而顯示的生滅諸法。本章以師父覺悟的心，來宣說俗諦中的十個主題。

這十個主題都屬於世俗諦的層面，因此對應於四法界中的事法界，所謂事法界者，如《華嚴經疏》云：

「理者。一真法界之性也。事者。一切世間之相也。」

《大明法數》云：

「事法界，謂諸眾生色心等法，一一差別，各有分齊，故名事法界。」

故本章之重點，在於針對世俗諦中種種的觀念加以智慧的詮釋。

海之章
毗盧性海歸體性　理事無礙心即佛

毗盧性海歸體性

此處之海，乃是毗盧性海，以海之相狀與體性呼應。此一性海，即法界緣起二分之一——「性海果分」，乃是相對於「普賢因分」而言。如《華嚴一乘教義分齊章》云：

「性海果分。是不可說義。何以故。不與教相應故。則十佛自境界也。」

本章的要點在於「心歸體性」，敘述師父所開示的入體性法門，也就是修心法要，故云「毗盧性海歸體性」。

理事無礙心即佛

本章對應於理事無礙法界，如《大明法數》云：

「理事無礙法界，謂理由事顯。事攬理成。理事互融。故名理事無礙法界。」

《華嚴法界玄鏡》云：

「理事無礙者。理無形相全在相中。互奪存亡故云無礙。」

本章由此意義，以喻於「心、性」，心屬於事，體性屬於理，心歸體性，性由心顯，心性互融，因此「理事無礙心即佛」，心佛無礙而互融，由此彰顯修心法門之奧秘。

天之章
虛空法身無言說　理法界中體性空

虛空法身無言說

此處之天，乃是「虛空法身」，如《華嚴經》云：

「汝等應觀佛所行。廣大寂靜虛空相。」

本章的要點在於「直指心性」、「直指法界」。乃是師父對於無言體性、心性的詮釋與證悟的描述，也就是對於無言的虛空法身起言說，故云「虛空法身無言說」。

理法界中體性空

此直指之心性，對應於四法界中之「理法界」，乃是真空之法界也。如《大明法數》云：

「理法界謂諸眾生色心等法。雖有差別。而同一體性。故名理法界。」

《華嚴法界玄鏡》云：

「真空則理法界二如本名。……言真空者。非斷滅空。非離色空。即有明空。亦無空相。故名真空。如文具之。」

由此故云：「理法界中體性空」。

人之章
普賢行願窮三際　事事無礙菩薩行

普賢行願窮三際

在《華嚴經》中，菩薩行之代表，乃是大普賢，整個法界緣起，無非是諸佛性海以及普賢菩薩二者之交融，如《華嚴一乘教義分齊章》云：

「夫法界緣起。乃自在無窮。今以要門略攝為二。一者明究竟果證義。即十佛自境界也。二者隨緣約因辯教義。即普賢境界也。」

是故本章以普賢菩薩，對應於「人」。

事事無礙菩薩行

本章以師父開示菩薩法門為主旨，對應於「事事無礙法界」，如《大明三藏法數》云：

「事事無礙法界，謂一切分齊事法。稱性融通。一多相即。大小互容。重重無盡。故名事事無礙法界。」

普賢十願，乃事事無礙法界力用之具體展現，其中總括一切菩薩行。乃是於眾生之事中行菩薩之事，以菩薩之事開覺眾生之心，是故菩薩行之根源，即事事無礙法界，故云「事事無礙菩薩行」。

Foreword

In this book the concept of "mountain, sea, sky, man" is used to express the "four realms of reality" of the Huayan school of Buddhism. Mountain corresponds to the realm of individual phenomena; sea corresponds to the realm of nonobstruction between principle and phenomena; sky corresponds to the realm of the one principle (śūnyatā) ; and man corresponds to the realm of nonobstruction between phenomena. The same correspondence is expressed in the following verse:

Mountain:

From the sacred mountain of Huayan, entering the realm of reality; conventional truth is spoken in the realm of individual phenomena.

Sea:

Returning to the essence through the sea of Vairocana; Buddha is the realm of nonobstruction between principle and phenomena.

Sky:

The universal Dharmakaya is ineffable; in the realm of the one principle the essential nature is emptiness itself.

Man:

The vows of Samantabhadra span the three times; the realm of nonobstruction between phenomena—this is the Bodhisattva practice.

Line one: Mountain

From the sacred mountain of Huayan, entering the realm of reality; conventional truth is spoken in the realm of individual phenomena.

From the sacred mountain of Huayan, entering the realm of reality;

Here "mountain" refers to Ling Jiou Mountain as a manifestation of the incomparably majestic sacred mountain of Huayan. This line expresses the wish that Ling Jiou Mountain will guide all sentient beings into the realm of reality.

Conventional truth is spoken in the realm of individual phenomena.

Here "conventional truth" refers to the arising and passing away of all phenomena that belong to the world of conventional reality, as described by Master Hsin Tao in his discourse on the ten aspects of conventional reality.

These ten aspects of conventional reality correspond to the realm of individual reality, as explained in the Commentary on the Huayan Sutra as follows:

"Principle" refers to the essential nature of the one impartial Dharma realm. "Phenomenon" refers to the appearance of everything in the world.

The *Daming fashu* states:

The "realm of individual reality" is so named because the beings which inhabit it differentiate all phenomena, both physical and mental, into individual objects of perception.

Thus this line reminds us to use wisdom when observing the myriad phenomena of the world.

Line two: Sea

Returning to the essence through the sea of Vairocana's nature; Buddha is the realm of nonobstruction between principle and phenomena.

Returning to the essence through the sea of Vairocana's nature;

Here the sea represents one's essential nature. The sea of one's essential nature refers to the ocean-like true nature of the effect aspect of dependent co-arising from the Dharma realm. As the *Huayan yisheng jiao fenqi zhang* states:

The ocean-like true nature of the effect aspect can't be taught, for it is ineffable. It is the state of the ten buddhas.

This line points out that returning to one's essential nature is the heart of spiritual practice.

Buddha is the realm of nonobstruction between principle and phenomena.

As for the "the realm of nonobstruction between principle and phenomena," the *Daming Fashu* states:

The realm of nonobstruction between principle and phenomena refers to the way in which principle manifests through phenomena, and phenomena come into being through principle. Thus principle and phenomena are interdependent.

The Huayan fajie xuanjing states:

The nonobstruction between principle and phenomena means that although principle is without form, it completely inheres in form.

The main idea of this line is that the mind is phenomenal, while essential nature belongs to principle. The mind returns to the essence, and the essence manifests through the mind; thus they are interpenetrating. Therefore, this line points out the interpenetrating nature of the mind and the Buddha.

Line three: Sky

The universal Dharmakaya is ineffable; in the realm of the one principle the essential nature is emptiness itself.

The universal Dharmakaya is ineffable;

Here, sky refers to the universal Dharmakaya, as thus explained in the Huayan Sutra:

You must contemplate all the Buddha's actions as the sign of quiescence, the sign of universal emptiness.

This line refers to the Dharmakaya and the nature of the mind, what Master Hsin Tao refers to as the ineffable essential nature of the mind.

In the realm of the one principle the essential nature is emptiness itself.

With respect to this essential nature, the *Daming Fashu* states:

The realm of the one principle comprises all the mental and physical phenomena of a sentient being. Although different, they are of the same nature.

The *Huayan fajie xuanjing* states:

True emptiness is not annihilation, nor is it apart from form. It is visible, yet devoid of attributes; thus it is called true emptiness.

Line four: Man

The vows of Samantabhadra span the three times; the realm of nonobstruction between phenomena—this is the bodhisattva practice.

The vows of Samantabhadra span the three times;

In the Huayan Sutra the Bodhisattva practice represents Samantabhadra. Dependent co-arising from the Dharma realm is nothing other than the interpenetration of the Buddha-nature and Samantabhadra, as thus explained in the *Huayan yisheng jiao yifen qizhang:*

This Dharma realm is dependently arisen; that's why it is boundless and inexhaustible. On the one hand, the result is insight into the independent state of the Buddhas; on the other hand, there is explication of the doctrine. This is the state of Samantabhadra.

Thus "man" in this line corresponds to the Bodhisattva Samantabhadra.

The realm of nonobstruction between phenomena—this is the Bodhisattva practice.

The Bodhisattva practice corresponds to the realm of nonobstruction between phenomena, as thus explained in the *Daming sanzang fashu:*

The realm of nonobstruction between phenomena refers to the interpenetrating nature of all phenomena; the identity of the one and the many; the inexhaustible interdependence of big and small.

The ten vows of Samantabhadra are a manifestation of the realm of nonobstruction between phenomena, and serve as an outline of the bodhisattva path. It's all about treading the Bodhisattva path in the world so as to lead all sentient beings towards awakening. Thus the realm of nonobstruction between phenomena is the wellspring of the Bodhisattva path.

華嚴聖山

The Holy Mountain of Avatamsaka

這山，
This mountain,

叫靈鷲山。
Is called Ling Jiou Mountain,

敍說著無盡生命的甘泉。
Narrating the sweet springs of infinite life.

業流

生命是什麼？
生命是基因組合。

基因是什麼？
基因是念頭而來的；
每一個念頭累積起來匯聚成業力，
業力累積起來就形成輪迴。

念頭從哪裡來呢？
念頭是從一切事事物物而來的。

一個個念頭的累積，變成了想法，
你的想法跟別人的想法匯流在一起，形成了業力；
想法會互相牽制，
互相牽制之中，生出一股相互的動力就是業力，
這反覆流動的業力，就是輪迴！

The Flow of Karma

What is life?
Life is the combination of genes.

What are genes?
Genes emerge from thought;
Every thought accumulates together to become Karma,
And the accumulation of Karma then results in reincarnation.

Where does thought come from?
It comes from all matters and things.

One after one thoughts accumulate and become concepts,
Your perception and other's perception converge together and form Karma;
Concepts restrain each other,
By restraining each other, a force of interaction originates, it is Karma;
And the repeated flow of Karma is called reincarnation.

The Flow of Karma

What is life?
Life is the combination of genes.

What are genes?
Genes emerge from thought;
Every thought accumulates together to become Karma,
And the accumulation of Karma then results in reincarnation.

Where does thought come from?
It comes from all matters and things.

One after one thoughts accumulate and become concepts,
Your perception and other's perception converge together and form Karma;
Concepts restrain each other.
By restraining each other, a force of interaction originates, it is Karma;
And the repeated flow of Karma is called reincarnation.

「天眼門」。

「天眼」指虛空之眼，取其澈見諸法空性之意；引領眾生進入心靈智慧的殿堂。

The Tianyan Gate at the main entrance to LJM. The "Divine Eyes" on top of the gate express the profound vision of emptiness in which all things are clearly discerned. The gate invites all to enter into the sanctuary of the heart of wisdom.

眾生

我們本來就是佛，
只是現在被種種的想法給蓋住了。

每一個人的心本來是光明的。
現在為什麼不光明呢？
起煩惱的時候，光明就沒有了，只看到煩惱；
起好壞的時候，光明就消失了，只看到好壞；
執著妄念之時，光明就不見了，被烏雲蓋住了，
這時，我們就不解脫、不光明了！

為什麼說我們都是佛，
可是卻還沒成佛？
這是因為沒有經歷過訓練——
那份認識自己的訓練，就叫做「修行」。

每個人的心性是不生不滅的，
如何去證明它呢？
禪修！
禪修會引導你不斷地發現、引導你回到自己！

Sentient Beings

We are Buddhas by nature,
It is only that we are now obscured by all kinds of concepts.

Every one's mind was originally radiant.
Why is it not radiant now?
When there is affliction, there is no radiance; we see only affliction.
When there is good and bad, radiance disappears; We see only good and bad.
When there is attachment to illusory thoughts,
radiance is gone, covered by dark clouds,
At this time, we are not free, not radiant anymore.

Why does it say that we are Buddhas,
but have not yet attained Buddhahood?
This is because we have not been trained.
The training of knowing your real self is called "Dharma Practice".

The nature of every one's mind is not arising and not ceasing.
How to prove it?
Meditate!
Meditation will guide you to constantly discover,
Guide you to return to your true self.

Sentient Beings

We are Buddhas by nature,
It is only that we are now obscured by all kinds of concepts.

Every one's mind was originally radiant.
Why is it not radiant now?
When there is affliction, there is no radiance; we see only affliction.
When there is good and bad, radiance disappears; We see only good and bad.
When there is attachment to illusory thoughts,
radiance is gone, covered by dark clouds,
At this time, we are not free, not radiant anymore.

Why does it say that we are Buddhas,
but have not yet attained Buddhahood?
This is because we have not been trained.
The training of knowing your real self is called "Dharma Practice".

The nature of every one's mind is not arising and not ceasing.
How to prove it?
Meditate!
Meditation will guide you to constantly discover,
Guide you to return to your true self.

「觀音道場」。
尋聲救苦的多羅觀音，慈眼視眾生、悲心度一切。

Guanyin Terrace.
Duoluo Guanyin surveys the world with eyes and ears of compassion and rescues beings in distress.

存在

什麼是寂靜呢？
就是安靜的聲音。

什麼是安靜的聲音呢？
就是沒有聲音。

身心就像流水一樣川流不息，
流在生生死死的大海，
每一個念頭、每一個想法都是流動的，
死亡與出生都是流動的，
一切的流動都是生滅的，
都是無常的，
沒有一個念頭是真實的。

放鬆每一個念頭，
靜靜地聽、安靜地聽，
聽寂靜——無聲之聲。

Existence

What is silence?
It's the sound of stillness.

What is the sound of stillness?
It is no sound at all.

Body and mind flow nonstop like running water,
Flowing in the ocean of death and rebirth.
All thoughts, all concepts are flowing.
Death and rebirth are flowing.
All that flows is subject to arising and ceasing,
Impermanent,
There is no one thought that is real.

Relax your every thought,
Listen silently, listen quietly,
Listen to the silence, the sound of no sound.

Existence

What is silence?
It's the sound of stillness.

What is the sound of stillness?
It is no sound at all.

Body and mind flow nonstop like running water,
Flowing in the ocean of death and rebirth.
All thoughts, all concepts are flowing.
Death and rebirth are flowing.
All that flows is subject to arising and ceasing,
Impermanent,
There is no one thought that is real.

Relax your every thought,
Listen silently, listen quietly,
Listen to the silence, the sound of no sound.

正覺塔內供奉九頭龍王護蓋的金佛像，
祈每位佛子都有悟道成正覺的願力。

Inside this replica of the Mahabodhi Stupa is a golden image of the Buddha sheltered by the nine-headed serpent king Mucalinda.
Pray that every child of the Buddha may awaken and accomplish the way.

生命

學習佛法，要把「因果」認識清楚，
「因」是從心的活動開始所想、所做的，
「果」就呈現在生活範圍、生活空間，
所看到的、所聽到的就叫「果」。

一切唯心所造、唯識所顯，
唯心所造就是因，
唯識所顯就是果。

心生了什麼念頭，
就會感召產生什麼樣的生命型態；
每一個眾生也都是自己的心念所顯、所形成的。

讓我們從耳根進入覺性，
從耳根找回自己的本來面目，
從耳根聆聽寂靜——
斷除一切的相，
也斷除一切的心。

Life

To learn Buddhist Dharma,
we have to have a clear understanding of cause and effect.
Thoughts and actions that have originated from the activity of the mind are "cause";
And "effect" will appear in the scope of our life,
What we see and hear is the "effect".

All phenomena are creations of the mind,
and manifestation of our own consciousness.
Creations of the mind are the cause,
Manifestation of our own consciousness is the effect.
Whatever thought that arises in the mind will impel
the relevant life form to come about;
Every sentient being is a manifestation,
A result of his/her own mind thought.

Let's enter our nature of awareness through the sense of hearing,
To find the face of our original self through the ears.
From our sense of hearing listen to the silence,
Abandon all forms,
Abandon all minds.

Life

To learn Buddhist Dharma,
we have to have a clear understanding of cause and effect.
Thoughts and actions that have originated from the activity of the mind are "cause";
And "effect" will appear in the scope of our life,
What we see and hear is the "effect".

All phenomena are creations of the mind,
and manifestation of our own consciousness.
Creations of the mind are the cause,
Manifestation of our own consciousness is the effect.
Whatever thought that arises in the mind will impel
the relevant life form to come about;
Every sentient being is a manifestation,
A result of his/her own mind thought.

Let's enter our nature of awareness through the sense of hearing,
To find the face of our original self through the ears.
From our sense of hearing listen to the silence,
Abandon all forms,
Abandon all minds.

唯心所造就是因，唯識所顯就是果。

The mind is both cause and effect.

轉生

每個人都會死，
「死」代表什麼？
對修行菩薩道的人來說，
死不過是一種方便。

這一生度了這麼多眾生，
到了另外一個地方，
把舊的身體丟掉，
轉換一個新的身體，
再結緣、再度眾生，
因此，「死」是不是方便？

「死」不是此生與來生的分界點，
它是一種方便，
就好像小孩子轉成大人的過程一般，
人死了，才能轉生，
轉生到另外一個世界的時候，
同樣是帶著願力跟慈悲而來。

Rebirth

Every one dies.
What does death represent?
For a practitioner following the Bodhisattva path,
Death is nothing but a skillful means.

One has enlightened so many sentient beings in this life,
It's time to go to another place,
Throw away the old body,
And change to a new one,
To continue making karmic connections and enlightening sentient beings.
So, isn't death a skillful means?

Death is not a point of demarcation between this life and future life.
It is an accommodation.
Just like the process of a child turning into an adult,
One has to die to be reborn again.
When one is born again in another world,
One still comes back with the same vows and compassion.

Rebirth

Every one dies.
What does death represent?
For a practitioner following the Bodhisattva path,
Death is nothing but a skillful means.

One has enlightened so many sentient beings in this life,
It's time to go to another place,
Throw away the old body,
And change to a new one,
To continue making karmic connections and enlightening sentient beings.
So, isn't death a skillful means?

Death is not a point of demarcation between this life and future life.
It is an accommodation.
Just like the process of a child turning into an adult,
One has to die to be reborn again.
When one is born again in another world,
One still comes back with the same vows and compassion.

「開山聖殿」。
殿中供奉緬甸國寶玉佛，現址為創寺的大殿所在。

The Jade Buddha from Myanmar in the Founders Hall.

當下

現下的生活就是淨土，
現下的生活就是福報，
現下的生活就是修行，
以這最現實的感覺，去做好它，
這也就是「現報」──現下的感受啊！

因果做好了，還害怕什麼呢？
我已經做好準備，絕對豐收，
輪迴與我又有何干呢？
我已經把未來的生命、命運創造出來。

命運隨時隨地掌握在你手裡，
你就是創造自己未來生命的主人，
不要等待，
這就是佛法。

In the Moment

The life of this moment is the Pure Land.
The life of this moment is the result of good merit.
The life of this moment is the Dharma practice.
Perceive the most real feeling and fulfill it,
This is the karmic result of this life - experience this present moment!
If the right "cause and effect" has been created,
what is there to be afraid of?

I am fully prepared, a bountiful harvest is definitely expected,
What does reincarnation have to do with me?
I have already created the future life, future destiny.

Destiny is always in your own hands,
You are the master of what is created in your future life,
Don't wait,
This is Dharma.

In the Moment

The life of this moment is the Pure Land.
The life of this moment is the result of good merit.
The life of this moment is the Dharma practice.
Perceive the most real feeling and fulfill it,
This is the karmic result of this life - experience this present moment!
If the right "cause and effect" has been created,
what is there to be afraid of?

I am fully prepared, a bountiful harvest is definitely expected,
What does reincarnation have to do with me?
I have already created the future life, future destiny.

Destiny is always in your own hands,
You are the master of what is created in your future life,
Don't wait,
This is Dharma.

「普賢道場」。
以巨石雕刻的佛足，象徵佛教修行的人生觀，實踐普賢願力。

These "Footprints of the Buddha" carved into a large boulder on the Samantabhadra Terrace give expression to the Buddhist outlook on life and spiritual practice.

意識

識是讓你去分別現象，
所以叫做「識別」。

如果安住在靈性上，就沒得分別了；
沒有任何東西可以讓你去分別，
在靈性上，你就越看越沒有，
越看心越收回、越收攝。

看著你的靈性，
無論生出什麼念頭都不要管它，
好好地看著靈性。

識附著在現象、觀念上，
捨棄觀念、捨棄著相生心，
識就會清淨。

識不清淨就會著相生心，
產生分別心。

識只是影像，一個幻影而已，
所以識不可得。

Consciousness

The function of consciousness is to discriminate phenomena,
It is known as "discrimination".

If we abide in our true nature, there will be no discrimination.
There is nothing to be discriminated.
When you are in true nature, the more you look, the less you will see.
And the more the mind will be concentrated and focused.

Look at your true nature,
No matter what thought has emerged from it, ignore it,
Just contemplate the true nature.

Consciousness adheres to phenomena, concepts,
Abandon concepts, abandon the mind that attaches to forms,
Our consciousness will become pure.

If consciousness is not pure, mind will attach to forms,
And discrimination arises.

Consciousness is just an image,
Just a mirage,
So consciousness is unobtainable.

Consciousness

The function of consciousness is to discriminate phenomena,
It is known as "discrimination."

If we abide in our true nature, there will be no discrimination.
There is nothing to be discriminated.
When you are in true nature, the more you look, the less you will see.
And the more the mind will be concentrated and focused.

Look at your true nature,
No matter what thought has emerged from it, ignore it,
Just contemplate the true nature.

Consciousness adheres to phenomena, concepts,
Abandon concepts, abandon the mind that attaches to forms,
Our consciousness will become pure.

If consciousness is not pure, mind will attach to forms,
And discrimination arises.

Consciousness is just an image,
Just a mirage,
So consciousness is unobtainable.

阿育王柱上雕有法輪、獅子和蓮花瓣，屹立莊嚴，象徵靈鷲山以弘揚佛法為志。

This replica of an Asokan pillar is topped with a lotus flower, a lion, and a wheel, representing LJM's mission of propagating the Dharma.

護生

愛惜生命，生命才會存活下去；
如果不愛生命，生命就被糟蹋掉。

一切眾生都愛護自己的生命，
連廁所裡面的蛆也不例外，
怕被人家殺死。

為什麼我們不愛惜自己的生命呢？
那是因為我們不曾認識生命的奇蹟，
不認識生命的感動與生命那份珍貴的動感。

眾生愛生命，諸佛慈愛眾生，
沒有一個眾生不愛自己的生命，
沒有一佛不愛眾生。

因為我們和眾生是相互連接的關係，
每個眾生是我們投生的地方，
每個眾生是我們的財富的所在，
每個眾生也是我們力量的來源。

愛護眾生就是愛護自己，
關懷自己的生命就是關懷一切的眾生。

Protecting Life

Cherish life, and life will continue to exist;
If we don't love life, it will be ruined.

Every sentient being loves to protect their own life,
Even the maggots in the toilet are not excluded,
They are also afraid of being killed.

Why don't we cherish our own life?
It is because we haven't understood the miracle of life,
Don't understand how life can move us and the precious rhythm of life.
Sentient beings love life, Buddhas love sentient beings with equanimity,
There is no sentient being that doesn't love their own life,
And there is no Buddha that doesn't love all sentient beings.

Because our relationship with all sentient beings is interconnected,
The form of all kinds of sentient beings is where we will be reborn,
The place of our fortune and wealth,
And the source of our strength.

To love and protect sentient beings is to love and protect oneself,
Caring for one's own life is caring for all sentient beings.

Protecting Life

Cherish life, and life will continue to exist;
If we don't love life, it will be ruined.

Every sentient being loves to protect their own life,
Even the maggots in the toilet are not excluded,
They are also afraid of being killed.

Why don't we cherish our own life?
It is because we haven't understood the miracle of life,
Don't understand how life can move us and the precious rhythm of life.
Sentient beings love life, Buddhas love sentient beings with equanimity,
There is no sentient being that doesn't love their own life,
And there is no Buddha that doesn't love all sentient beings.

Because our relationship with all sentient beings is interconnected,
The form of all kinds of sentient beings is where we will be reborn,
The place of our fortune and wealth,
And the source of our strength.

To love and protect sentient beings is to love and protect oneself,
Caring for one's own life is caring for all sentient beings.

法輪雙鹿，代表佛法長存、法輪常轉。

The wheel of the Dharma flanked by two deer, representing the Buddha's first sermon at the Deer Park and the continuity of the teaching.

身體

身體是唯心造、唯識顯出來的，
心造作了業，
隨著業力牽引成為一個形體，
變成這個身體。

心造作了今生的身體，
造作來生的身體，
也會造生生世世的身體，
在這造作的無窮無盡身體裡，
誰是我？
哪一個是我？
生生世世的身體都是我們的心所造的，
到底哪一個是我呢？

The Body

The body is a creation of mind, a manifestation of consciousness,
The mind creates karma,
And with the karmic force brings about a form,
Which becomes our body.

Mind creates the body of this life,
The body of the next life,
And the bodies of life after life,
In those bodies which have been created endlessly,
Who am I?
Which one is I?
The bodies of life after life are all created by our mind,
In the end, which one is I?

The Body

The body is a creation of mind, a manifestation of consciousness,
The mind creates karma,
And with the karmic force brings about a form,
Which becomes our body.

Mind creates the body of this life,
The body of the next life,
And the bodies of life after life,
In those bodies which have been created endlessly,
Who am I?
Which one is I?
The bodies of life after life are all created by our mind,
In the end, which one is I?

金佛殿圓形建築象徵圓融、圓滿的華嚴世界，
其上的金剛鈴杵與寶瓶，彰顯心道法師三乘圓融之特色。

The circular shape of the Golden Buddha Hall represents the perfection and unity of the Huayan Realm.
The *vajra* and vase forming the peak of the hall indicate the integration of the three schools of Buddhism at LJM.

因果

輪迴是念頭相續而成的，
每一個念頭都很重要的！
就像下賭注一樣，
賭下去就是輸贏，
每個念頭都要很小心，
因為每起一個念頭就是輸贏！

「因」就是每一個起心動念，
「果」就是感受環境、人、事、物，
對於外境好好壞壞的感受就是果。

「因」就是隨著現在產生的想法，
是好是壞，很快就回饋你相同的感受，
起心動念是「因」，
這種感受就是「果」。
所以佛法重視的是改變因果。

Cause and Effect

Reincarnation comes from continuous thoughts,
Every thought is important!
Just like making a bet,
Each bet results in a win or a loss;
Every thought needs to be made with care,
Because every thought that arises results in a win or a loss.

"Cause" is every thought that arises from the mind,
"Effect" is the perception of environment, people, matters and things,
The perception of good and bad in the external environment is "effect".

"Cause" is if one follows the present conception,
Perceiving good and bad,
quickly the same perception will come back to you,
The thought that arises from the mind is "cause",
And the perception is "effect".
Therefore Buddha Dharma emphasizes changing "cause and effect".

Cause and Effect

Reincarnation comes from continuous thoughts,
Every thought is important!
Just like making a bet,
Each bet results in a win or a loss;
Every thought needs to be made with care,
Because every thought that arises results in a win or a loss.

"Cause" is every thought that arises from the mind,
"Effect" is the perception of environment, people, matters and things,
The perception of good and bad in the external environment is "effect".

"Cause" is it one follows the present conception,
Perceiving good and bad,
quickly the same perception will come back to you,
The thought that arises from the mind is "cause",
And the perception is "effect".
Therefore Buddha Dharma emphasizes changing "cause and effect".

金佛殿內供奉三尊泰國金佛，
圓頂的華嚴字母，象徵華嚴智慧的殊勝境界。

Enshrined in the Golden Buddha Hall are three golden Buddhas from Thailand.
The Siddham letters on the ceiling represent the perfect wisdom of the Huayan Realm.

毗盧性海

The Vairocana Ocean of Reality

這海，
This ocean,

叫做般若海。
Is called the Ocean of Prajna,

吹動著識浪，
The wind moves the waves of consciousness,

經驗著生死，
Experiencing life and death,

終歸於平息的大海。
However, it will eventually return to a calm and peaceful ocean.

放鬆

修行，
就是讓你的心，
在任何起煩惱的地方放鬆，
放鬆就是止、休歇，就是歇息啊！

什麼是修行呢？
當你執著的時候，
這時也就是你放鬆的時候。
放鬆的時候就是大修行。

在生活裡面，
起了執著心，
起了貪心、瞋心、癡心的時候，
學會放鬆，
放鬆就是一種離相。

Relaxation

Dharma practice,
Is to let your mind,
Relax in any place where afflictions arise;
Relaxation is to stop and take a break, just to be still and rest!

What is Dharma practice?
When you are attached,
It is the time when you should relax.
The great Dharma practice is when you are relaxed.

In our life,
When attachments arise,
When desire, hatred and ignorance arise,
Learn to relax,
Relaxation is the detachment from forms.

Relaxation

Dharma practice,
Is to let your mind,
Relax in any place where afflictions arise;
Relaxation is to stop and take a break, just to be still and rest!

What is Dharma practice?
When you are attached,
It is the time when you should relax.
The great Dharma practice is when you are relaxed.

In our life,
When attachments arise,
When desire, hatred and ignorance arise,
Learn to relax,
Relaxation is the detachment from forms.

在生活中學會放鬆，放鬆就是一種離相。

Learn to relax in the midst of life by not attaching to things.

心源

佛法之中法門雖多，
總攝歸於心。
如果沒有心，也沒有百千種法門，
因為百千種法門還是同源一心。

我們要證悟、要證果，
都要從心的總持去啟開、明白。

心統攝一切的法門。
心搞定了，一切都定了；
心沒有搞定，都是畫蛇添足，
這叫做心外求法，無一是處。

萬教、萬法、萬宗，
總不離開一個心的總持。
所以學法，要從心下手，
不從心下手，叫做多此一舉！

「百千法門，同歸方寸，河沙妙德，總在心源。」
這是禪宗四祖的開示，
告訴我們：心是一切保障、
心是一切法門、
心是一切能量。

The Origin of Mind

In the Buddha Dharma even though there are many Dharma gates,
The final focus comes back to the mind.
If there is no mind,
there would not be hundreds of thousand of Dharma gates,
Because hundreds of thousands of Dharma gates still have the same origin – mind.

We want to be enlightened, to become accomplished in the way
We have to use the power of mind to open up and understand.

Mind reins over all the Dharma gates,
Once the mind is settled, everything is settled;
If the mind is not settled, everything is unnecessarily complicated,
This so called searching for Dharma outside the mind,
there is nothing to be found.
Ten thousand teachings, ten thousand laws, ten thousand sects,
Can never exceed the power of mind.
Therefore to study the Dharma, we need to start with our mind,
If we don't start from our mind, then our efforts will be pointless.

"Hundreds of thousands of Dharma gates all return to One,
Infinite wonderful virtues are all originated from the mind."
This is the teaching of the Fourth Patriarch of Chan,
It is telling us:
Mind is every assurance,
Mind is every Dharma gate,
Mind is every energy.

The Origin of Mind

In the Buddha Dharma even though there are many Dharma gates,
The final focus comes back to the mind.
If there is no mind,
there would not be hundreds of thousand of Dharma gates,
Because hundreds of thousands of Dharma gates still have the same origin – mind.

We want to be enlightened, to become accomplished in the way
We have to use the power of mind to open up and understand.

Mind reins over all the Dharma gates,
Once the mind is settled, everything is settled;
If the mind is not settled, everything is unnecessarily complicated,
This so called searching for Dharma outside the mind,
there is nothing to be found.
Ten thousand teachings, ten thousand laws, ten thousand sects,
Can never exceed the power of mind.
Therefore to study the Dharma, we need to start with our mind,
If we don't start from our mind, then our efforts will be pointless.

"Hundreds of thousands of Dharma gates all return to One,
Infinite wonderful virtues are all originated from the mind."
This is the teaching of the Fourth Patriarch of Chan,
It is telling us:
Mind is every assurance,
Mind is every Dharma gate,
Mind is every energy.

百千法門，同歸方寸；心是一切法門、一切能量。

The innumerable Dharma doors all return to the heart.
The heart is the door to the Dharma, the source of inspiration.

安心

暢流無阻，
這是禪宗的心。
禪者的心，就是平平常常的過日子，
所以在生活中能夠安心。

如何安心呢？
就是不要去安心，
不用刻意找一個安心的地方去安心。

我們的心啊！
常常爲了錢而安心，
爲了感情而安心，
爲了事業而安心，
爲了買一間房子而安心，
爲了討小老婆而安心，
或者是找一個男朋友而安心。

安心，
是不必去找尋安心所在的，
所以你就不會爲了安心而被束縛。

Mind at Ease

Flowing freely without any obstacles,
This is the mind of Chan.
The mind of the Chan practitioner is to lead a very ordinary life,
Therefore the mind can be at ease in daily life.

How to ease your mind?
It is not trying to ease your mind,
Not to deliberately looking for a secure place to ease your mind.

Ah, our mind!
It often looks for money to ease the mind,
Looks for feelings to ease the mind,
Looks for a career to ease the mind,
Looks to buy a house to ease the mind,
Looks for a mistress to ease the mind,
Or looks for a boyfriend to ease the mind.

Ease your mind,
No need to look for a place to ease your mind,
Therefore you will not be bound by trying to ease the mind.

Mind at Ease

Flowing freely without any obstacles,
This is the mind of Chan.
The mind of the Chan practitioner is to lead a very ordinary life,
Therefore the mind can be at ease in daily life.

How to ease your mind?
It is not trying to ease your mind,
Not to deliberately looking for a secure place to ease your mind.

Ah, our mind!
It often looks for money to ease the mind,
Looks for feelings to ease the mind,
Looks for a career to ease the mind,
Looks to buy a house to ease the mind,
Looks for a mistress to ease the mind,
Or looks for a boyfriend to ease the mind.

Ease your mind,
No need to look for a place to ease your mind,
Therefore you will not be bound by trying to ease the mind.

舍利塔林。佛塔建築造型各異，體現靈鷲山三乘法教。

The various shapes of the stupas in the Stupa Forest represent
the integration of the three schools of Buddhism at LJM.

三寶

我們擁有很多輪迴的本錢──貪、瞋、癡，
一天到晚就只想修這個，
沒有覺照自己的靈性，
沒有安住自己的靈性，
沒有清淨地看到自己的靈性，
因此就這樣輪迴。

「修行」，要怎麼修呢？
就是要念佛──念覺性，
念法──將心安住在法之覺性上。
念僧──安住在自己清淨覺性上。

看到覺性、安住在覺性上，
在這清淨覺性上生活，
就叫做──念佛、念法、念僧。

The Three Jewels

We own a lot of capital for reincarnation – greed, hatred and ignorance,
We practice these all day long,
Without illuminating our true nature,
Without abiding in our true nature,
Without purely seeing our true nature,
Therefore we just reincarnate like this.

How to practice "Dharma practice"?
We must contemplate Buddha – to contemplate our true nature,
Contemplate Dharma – to contemplate the true nature of Dharma,
Contemplate Sangha – to abide in the pure nature of our self.

To see our true nature, to abide in our true nature,
And to live in our pure true nature,
This is called contemplating Buddha, Dharma, Sangha.

The Three Jewels

We own a lot of capital for reincarnation – greed, hatred and ignorance,
We practice these all day long,
Without illuminating our true nature,
Without abiding in our true nature,
Without purely seeing our true nature,
Therefore we just reincarnate like this.

How to practice "Dharma practice"?
We must contemplate Buddha – to contemplate our true nature,
Contemplate Dharma – to contemplate the true nature of Dharma,
Contemplate Sangha – to abide in the pure nature of our self.

To see our true nature, to abide in our true nature,
And to live in our pure true nature,
This is called contemplating Buddha, Dharma, Sangha.

念佛、念法、念僧，在清淨覺性上生活。

Maintain mindfulness of the Triple Gem; live a life of awareness.

禪味

禪修可以除去習氣、堅定道心，
讓我們不斷地在菩薩道上前進。
因為有信心，我們不會退轉；
沒有信心，就會左顧右盼，
學法也就進進退退。

禪修是一種堅固——道心的堅固，
越坐，你越坐出味道來。
沒坐，味道就五味雜陳，
反而感覺不出那單純的味。

坐禪就是體會單純的味啊！
心性的味道、
安定的味道、
內心明亮的味道。

所以要有恆心地去觀照呼吸，
讓心與呼吸相互地呈現出心的光明。

The Flavour of Chan

The practice of Chan can eliminate our habitual tendencies,
to solidify our determination,
To let us continually make progress on the Bodhisattva path.
Because of our faith, we will not regress;
Without faith we will always look around with uncertainty,
And move backwards and forwards on the path of Dharma learning.

The practice of Chan is one kind of solidity –
The solidity of determination to practice Dharma,
The longer one sits, the more the flavour of Dharma comes.
If you don't sit, then the flavour of your mind is mixed up and confused,
Then you cannot taste that pure and simple flavour.
Meditation is to experience the flavour of simplicity,
The flavour of the nature of mind,
The flavour of stability,
And the flavour of inner radiance.

Therefore you need to illuminate the inhalation and exhalation with perseverance,
To make the mind and breath come together to reveal the radiance of mind.

The Flavour of Chan

The practice of Chan can eliminate our habitual tendencies,
to solidify our determination,
To let us continually make progress on the Bodhisattva path.
Because of our faith, we will not regress;
Without faith we will always look around with uncertainty,
And move backwards and forwards on the path of Dharma learning.

The practice of Chan is one kind of solidity –
The solidity of determination to practice Dharma,
The longer one sits, the more the flavour of Dharma comes.
If you don't sit, then the flavour of your mind is mixed up and confused,
Then you cannot taste that pure and simple flavour.
Meditation is to experience the flavour of simplicity,
The flavour of the nature of mind,
The flavour of stability,
And the flavour of inner radiance.

Therefore you need to illuminate the inhalation and exhalation with perseverance,
To make the mind and breath come together to reveal the radiance of mind.

藉由禪修堅固道心，讓心與呼吸呈現光明。

Meditation sets you firmly on the path; it brightens your heart and your breath.

空性

空是什麼呢？
怎麼會空呢？
怎麼能空呢？

空的意思是說，
我們儲存的這些思惟，
它只是影像，
它不是永恆的，
它是無常的，
它是幻覺的。

所以不要去執著這些如幻的事情，
把它給清理掉，
一旦執著，
貪、瞋、癡就會生起來。

Emptiness

What is emptiness?
How could it be empty?
How to be empty?

The meaning of emptiness is that,
The thoughts we store,
They are only an image,
They are not eternal,
They are impermanent,
They are illusory.

Don't get attached to those illusory things,
Clean them all up,
Once there is attachment,
Greed, hatred, ignorance will arise.

Emptiness

What is emptiness?
How could it be empty?
How to be empty?

The meaning of emptiness is that,
The thoughts we store,
They are only an image,
They are not eternal,
They are impermanent,
They are illusory.

Don't get attached to those illusory things,
Clean them all up,
Once there is attachment,
Greed, hatred, ignorance will arise.

不貪戀執著，凡所有相，皆是虛妄。

Be done with attachment, for all conditioned things are ephemeral.

聆聽

用耳根去聽，離心意識，
離心的做作，離意的分別，離識的作用，
心才能如秋天的天空一樣清朗明潔，
才能夠理解到法身如同「晴空萬里無片雲」。

當我們死亡，在進入一片黑暗以後，
光明會重現，
在藍色的光明中，會有法身的顯現，
在這光明當中，
自然息滅相對的一切。

用耳朵無分別地去聆聽，
在不二的空性之中，
聆聽安住，安靜聆聽，聆聽寂靜。

Listening

Listen with the sense of hearing, detach from the
mind, thinking and consciousness,
Detach from the creation of mind,
The discrimination of thinking,
And the function of consciousness,
Only then can the mind be clear and bright like the Autumn sky,
And one can then truly understand
the Dharmakaya is like a "vast cloudless sky".

When we are dead, after entering a state of darkness,
Radiance will appear again,
In the blue radiance, Dharmakaya will manifest,
In this radiance,
All that is relative will naturally cease.

Use the ears to listen with no discrimination,
Abide in the non-duality of emptiness,
Listen to the abiding, listen quietly, listen to the silence.

Listening

Listen with the sense of hearing, detach from the
mind, thinking and consciousness,
Detach from the creation of mind,
The discrimination of thinking,
And the function of consciousness,
Only then can the mind be clear and bright like the Autumn sky,
And one can then truly understand
the Dharmakaya is like a "vast cloudless sky".

When we are dead, after entering a state of darkness,
Radiance will appear again,
In the blue radiance, Dharmakaya will manifest,
In this radiance,
All that is relative will naturally cease.

Use the ears to listen with no discrimination,
Abide in the non-duality of emptiness,
Listen to the abiding, listen quietly, listen to the silence.

用耳根聆聽寂靜，離心意識，
讓法身晴空萬里。

Use the hearing faculty to listen to
silence; the mind of non-
discrimination is the bright and
boundless sky of the Dharmakaya.

覺性

尋找覺性，有時候是不太容易的，
因為這是一念之差的問題；
一念之悟，覺性就在那裡，
但是你就是沒有辦法體會。

所以要常常打坐，
從打坐中呈現靜相──安靜的相，
從靜相裡面才能反照出覺性。

天天使用覺性，
可是你就不知道它長得怎麼樣，
老是錯把它當成是這個身體，
事實上，它不是身體。
一定要離開身體去看、離開現象去看，
才可以看到這不生不滅的覺性。

覺性是不生不滅，
你如果在現象裡面看，
怎麼看也是身體，
怎麼看也是眼、耳、鼻、舌、身、意，
所以找覺性不容易。

其實找覺性也很容易，
叫做清清楚楚、明明白白，
這就是覺性。

Nature of Awareness

Searching for the nature of awareness, is not always easy,
Because the problematic thing is that one thought makes everything different;
One thought of awakening,
Is where the nature of awareness can be found,
But one cannot easily realize this.

So one must frequently practice meditation,
In meditation tranquility arises – the form of silence,
From this tranquility the nature of awareness can be reflected.

Every day one uses the nature of awareness,
But one just doesn't know what it looks like,
One always mistakes the body as the awareness,
In fact awareness is not the body.
One must detach from the body to see, detach from phenomena to see,
And then one can see the not arising and not ceasing nature of awareness.

The nature of awareness is not arising and not ceasing,
If one looks at phenomena,
One can only see the body,
One can only see the eye, ear, nose, tongue, body and mind,
So searching for the nature of awareness is not easy.

Actually searching for the nature of awareness is also easy,
When one is clearly aware of everything,
This is the nature of awareness.

Nature of Awareness

Searching for the nature of awareness, is not always easy,
Because the problematic thing is that one thought makes everything different;
One thought of awakening,
Is where the nature of awareness can be found,
But one cannot easily realize this.

So one must frequently practice meditation,
In meditation tranquility arises – the form of silence,
From this tranquility the nature of awareness can be reflected.

Every day one uses the nature of awareness,
But one just doesn't know what it looks like,
One always mistakes the body as the awareness,
In fact awareness is not the body.
One must detach from the body to see, detach from phenomena to see,
And then one can see the not arising and not ceasing nature of awareness.

The nature of awareness is not arising and not ceasing,
If one looks at phenomena,
One can only see the body,
One can only see the eye, ear, nose, tongue, body and mind,
So searching for the nature of awareness is not easy.

Actually searching for the nature of awareness is also easy,
When one is clearly aware of everything,
This is the nature of awareness.

覺性是不生不滅，清清楚楚、明明白白。

Enlightenment means clarity and understanding;
it neither arises nor ceases.

無我

無我不是沒有我，
因為沒有了假我，
呈現出真我才是真的快樂。

什麼是真我呢？
就是照破假我。

學習佛法，
以無常看待生命，
用無常看待一切事情的發生，
這些發生都是短暫的，
因為短暫，所以不真實，
因為不真實，所以我們不需要生起對立。

所謂無我，就是「我」常常變來變去，
今生是人，來生不曉得投生成什麼，
生命型態不停變化。

不管變成什麼型態，
生命總是短暫的，
最重要是去結廣大的善緣。

Non-self

Non-self is not no self,
Because when there is no false self,
Then the true self will arise,
This is the true happiness.

What is the true self?
It is to illuminate and break through the false self.

Study the Dharma,
Use the view of impermanence to see life,
Use the view of impermanence to see everything that happens,
Everything that happens is temporary,
Because it is temporary, it is not real,
Because it is not real, there is no need to create opposition.

The so called non-self, is that "I" is frequently changing,
In this life one is human,
But one doesn't know what they will be reborn as in the future life,
The form of life is constantly changing.

No matter what kind of form one becomes,
Life is always short,
The most important thing is to make a boundless,
Virtuous karmic connection.

Non-self

Non-self is not no self,
Because when there is no false self,
Then the true self will arise,
This is the true happiness.

What is the true self?
It is to illuminate and break through the false self.

Study the Dharma,
Use the view of impermanence to see life,
Use the view of impermanence to see everything that happens,
Everything that happens is temporary,
Because it is temporary, it is not real,
Because it is not real, there is no need to create opposition.

The so called non-self, is that "I" is frequently changing,
In this life one is human,
But one doesn't know what they will be reborn as in the future life,
The form of life is constantly changing.

No matter what kind of form one becomes,
Life is always short,
The most important thing is to make a boundless,
Virtuous karmic connection.

以無常看待一切，不生起對立。

Regarding all things as impermanent, opposition and conflict have nowhere to arise.

休息

如果沒有辦法體會如來的覺性，
就來練習平安禪，
聆聽寂靜，讓心安靜。

在寂靜中不被干擾，
慢慢從寂靜的明亮之中，
點燃法性的光明。

我教大家的就是「聆聽寂靜的光明」，
聆聽寂靜的目的是覺性，而不在寂靜。
是引領覺性的一個專注力，
讓我們能時常安住在覺性光明中──
覺性光明界中休息。

聆聽寂靜，
讓心不攀緣，不環扣一切妄念，
能夠息心淨念，住於覺性。

Resting

If one cannot truly understand the awareness of Tathagata,
Then one can practice tranquility meditation,
Listen to the silence, make the mind calm and quiet.

In the silence don't be disturbed,
Slowly from the brightness of the silence,
Light up the radiance of Dharmakaya.

What I teach everybody is "listen to the radiance of the silence",
The purpose of listening to the silence is the awareness, not the silence.
Silence is one kind of concentration that leads one to awareness,
It makes one abide in the radiance of awareness all the time,
To rest in the realm of the radiance of awareness.

Listen to the silence,
Make the mind free of clinging to forms or connecting to illusory thoughts,
Rest the mind and purify one's thoughts, abide in awareness.

Resting

If one cannot truly understand the awareness of Tathagata,
Then one can practice tranquility meditation,
Listen to the silence, make the mind calm and quiet.

In the silence don't be disturbed,
Slowly from the brightness of the silence,
Light up the radiance of Dharmakaya.

What I teach everybody is "listen to the radiance of the silence",
The purpose of listening to the silence is the awareness, not the silence.
Silence is one kind of concentration that leads one to awareness,
It makes one abide in the radiance of awareness all the time,
To rest in the realm of the radiance of awareness.

Listen to the silence,
Make the mind free of clinging to forms or connecting to illusory thoughts,
Rest the mind and purify one's thoughts, abide in awareness.

安住覺性，點燃法性光明。

Dwell in awareness; ignite the lamp of truth.

覺性天空

The Space of Awareness

這天，
This space,

叫大圓滿。
Is called the great perfection.

看作內，叫天眼門。
Take it as your inner world, it's called Gate of the Buddha Eye.

看作心，叫大手印。
Take it as your mind, it's called Mahamudra.

心即是禪

我們的心性即是禪。
禪是什麼？
禪就是真如實性。

在禪修中，
我們聽到了心聲，
體會了心、覺悟了心，
在一片寧靜當中，
感覺到就像佛在說法一般。

但是禪是什麼呢？
「禪」是不可得、不可說、不貪住、不執著。
無所得的心才是禪的心。
內心無所得才是禪的心境。

The Mind is Chan

The nature of our mind is Chan.
What is Chan?
Chan is the true form of suchness.

In meditation,
We hear the sound of our mind,
When we experience the mind, awaken the mind,
In a state of tranquility,
It feels just like the Buddha is giving Dharma talks.

But what is Chan?
Chan is unobtainable, unspeakable, not abiding with greed, not clinging.
The unobtainable mind is the mind of Chan.
The inner mind obtains nothing, this is a stage of Chan.

The Mind is Chan

The nature of our mind is Chan.
What is Chan?
Chan is the true form of suchness.

In meditation,
We hear the sound of our mind,
When we experience the mind, awaken the mind,
In a state of tranquility,
It feels just like the Buddha is giving Dharma talks.

But what is Chan?
Chan is unobtainable, unspeakable, not abiding with greed, not clinging.
The unobtainable mind is the mind of Chan.
The inner mind obtains nothing, this is a stage of Chan.

慈悲是生命的泉源活水，效法觀音濟度眾生的悲心大願。

Compassion is the wellspring of life; emulate the great compassion of Guanyin.

本來面目

我在閉黑關的時候，
「黑關」就是關房裡沒有任何光明，只是黑暗，
整個都看不到光，
卻有一個東西很明、很亮。
那是什麼？
對！自己的心性很明、很亮！
一直看，從這裡慢慢地看到本來的面目。

在黑暗裡面什麼都不亮，只有呼吸最亮，
在觀呼吸裡面，看到自己的本來面目。

要一直修下去，
這不是你修一下子就發現——
「噢！本來面目！」
那是不可能的。

The Original Face

When I stayed in a darkness retreat,
"Darkness retreat" means staying in a room without any light, it is totally dark,
I couldn't see any light at all,
But there was one thing very bright and radiant.
What was that?
Right! Our own mind nature is very bright and radiant!
Keep looking, from here one can slowly see one's original face.

In the darkness there is nothing light, only the breath is bright,
Through observing the breath, one can see one's original face.

Continuously practice meditation,
It is not something you can do in a moment and discover –
Oh! My original face!
That is impossible.

The Original Face

When I stayed in a darkness retreat,
"Darkness retreat" means staying in a room without any light, it is totally dark,
I couldn't see any light at all.
But there was one thing very bright and radiant.
What was that?
Right! Our own mind nature is very bright and radiant!
Keep looking, from here one can slowly see one's original face.

In the darkness there is nothing light, only the breath is bright,
Through observing the breath, one can see one's original face.

Continuously practice meditation,
It is not something you can do in a moment and discover –
Oh! My original face!
That is impossible.

自性光明，看到自己的本來面目。

Use your bright essential nature to observe your original face.

核心能量

佛就是宇宙！
是一種核心的能量，
祂的能量，
是一種充滿愛心的能量。
能夠覺醒眾生，而且使眾生充滿能量。

每個人都具足這種核心能量，
只是，還沒學佛之前，
我們的思想、行為，是外在的，
而不是核心的。

如果可以覺悟佛法，
生命就會轉化成核心的能量，
這種能量，是整個宇宙的動力。

學佛，
就可以啟動這核心能量的快樂、離苦。

The Core Energy

Buddha is the universe!
A kind of core energy,
His energy,
Is an energy full of love,
It can awaken sentient beings, and make them full of love.

Every person has this kind of core energy,
However, before we have studied the Dharma,
Our thoughts and actions are external,
And not from the core.

If we can awaken to the Dharma,
Life can transform to the core energy,
This energy is the power of the entire universe.

Practice the Buddha Dharma,
One can fire up the core energy,
Its happiness and freedom from suffering.

The Core Energy

Buddha is the universe!
A kind of core energy,
His energy,
Is an energy full of love,
It can awaken sentient beings, and make them full of love.

Every person has this kind of core energy,
However, before we have studied the Dharma,
Our thoughts and actions are external,
And not from the core.

If we can awaken to the Dharma,
Life can transform to the core energy,
This energy is the power of the entire universe.

Practice the Buddha Dharma,
One can fire up the core energy,
Its happiness and freedom from suffering.

佛的能量充滿愛心，而能夠覺醒眾生。

The power of the Buddha is imbued with love,
and has the capacity to lead others to awakening.

永恆歸宿

人生如夢如幻啊！
在任何地方，
感覺到生命是那麼的短暫，
所以必須找尋真理，
找尋永恆的歸宿處。

什麼是永恆的歸宿處呢？
就是我們的覺性、空性。

覺性、空性，
不隨生滅而生滅，
不隨因緣而變化，
不隨現象起伏而變化，
所以是不來不去、不垢不淨、不生不滅的。

不執著情境的變化，
安靜地聆聽，事事物物生滅變化，
這些生滅變化，終究會寂滅。

所以我們要任持寂滅性，
不變不動、不取不捨，
讓我們的心安住在明明朗朗，
安住在清清楚楚、無罣無礙的廣大空間。

Eternal Home

Life is like a dream, a mirage!
In any place,
We feel that life is so short,
So we must search for the truth,
Search for the eternal home.

What is the eternal home?
It is just our nature of awareness and emptiness.

The nature of awareness, emptiness,
It doesn't follow the arising or ceasing,
It doesn't change according to the conditions,
It doesn't change according to the rising and falling of phenomena,
Therefore it is not coming or going,
Not defiled or pure, not arising or ceasing.
Not clinging to the changing of the conceptual environment,
Listen quietly, matters and things arise and cease and change,
All this will eventually disappear in silence.

Therefore we need to recognize the nature of cessation,
Not changing, not moving, not grasping, not renouncing,
Let our mind abide in the brightness,
Abide in clearness, abide in vast space that is free of obstacles.

Eternal Home

Life is like a dream, a mirage!
In any place,
We feel that life is so short,
So we must search for the truth,
Search for the eternal home.

What is the eternal home?
It is just our nature of awareness and emptiness.

The nature of awareness, emptiness,
It doesn't follow the arising or ceasing,
It doesn't change according to the conditions,
It doesn't change according to the rising and falling of phenomena,
Therefore it is not coming or going,
Not defiled or pure, not arising or ceasing.
Not clinging to the changing of the conceptual environment,
Listen quietly, matters and things arise and cease and change.
All this will eventually disappear in silence.

Therefore we need to recognize the nature of cessation,
Not changing, not moving, not grasping, not renouncing,
Let our mind abide in the brightness,
Abide in clearness, abide in vast space that is free of obstacles.

覺性，不來不去、不垢不淨、不生不滅。

That which neither comes nor goes, is neither pure nor impure,
neither arises nor ceases—that is enlightenment.

安住持明

密宗有所謂的持明尊。
什麼是「持明」呢？
人的特點，
就是有一個無所不在的持明功能，
像電燈一樣能夠照明，
累劫、累生、累世都是這樣子，
沒有改變過；
出生的時候，就是這樣子，
死亡的時候，也沒有離開過這份持明功能。

回到本有的持明功能，
把這些著相的心念，
慢慢地從持明中消除、消失，
我們就能很清楚地覺明。

常常將心如是安住，
安住在離相的持明境界，
離一切幻有執著的持明境界，
離一切我執、法執的持明境界。

Abiding in Illumination

Vajrayana has illumination deities.
What is illumination?
The special feature of humans,
Is that there is one kind of illuminating function which is everywhere,
It can illuminate like an electric light,
Even through accumulated eons of time, accumulated lives it is still like this,
It has never changed;
It is like this when we are born,
Even when we die, we have not been apart from this illuminating function.

Returning to the original illuminating function,
When we are in the illumination,
Gradually we eliminate and destroy the mind thoughts that are attached to forms,
We can clearly be aware and luminous.

Frequently abide the mind in such a way,
Abide in the illuminating stage of abandoning forms,
Abandon all the attachments of illusory existence,
Abandon the attachment to self and the attachment to Dharma.

Abiding in Illumination

Vajrayana has illumination deities.
What is illumination?
The special feature of humans,
Is that there is one kind of illuminating function which is everywhere,
It can illuminate like an electric light,
Even through accumulated eons of time, accumulated lives it is still like this,
It has never changed;
It is like this when we are born,
Even when we die, we have not been apart from this illuminating function.

Returning to the original illuminating function,
When we are in the illumination,
Gradually we eliminate and destroy the mind thoughts that are attached to forms,
We can clearly be aware and luminous.

Frequently abide the mind in such a way,
Abide in the illuminating stage of abandoning forms,
Abandon all the attachments of illusory existence,
Abandon the attachment to self and the attachment to Dharma.

將心安住，安住在離相的持明境界。

Settling the mind into the state of non-attachment represented by the mantra.

離相眞如

妄念是什麼呢？就是現象。
心念因爲現象而形成妄念；
心念離相，即是「眞如」。

眞如遍一切處，
因爲遍一切處，
所以眞如即是一切法，
一切法即是眞如。

離念、息念、離相，
離念就是息念，
息念就是眞如，
眞如是如如不二，
不二就是沒有對立、沒有相對。

禪修、聆聽寂靜，
讓我們離一切的妄念，
離妄成眞，進入實相。

眞如即是實相，
實相則無不相。

Abandon Forms, True Suchness

What is illusory thought? It is phenomena.
Illusory thought arises from the mind because of phenomena;
Mind abandons forms, that is "true suchness".

True suchness fills all space,
Because it fills all space,
True suchness is every Dharma,
Every Dharma is true suchness.

Abandon thoughts, cease thoughts, abandon forms,
Abandoning thoughts is ceasing thoughts,
Ceasing thoughts is true suchness,
True suchness is the suchness of non-duality,
Non-duality is without opposition or relativity.

Meditate, listen to the silence,
Let us abandon every illusory thought,
Abandoning illusion turn to truth, enter the form of the absolute truth.

True suchness is absolute truth,
Absolute truth is in every form.

Abandon Forms, True Suchness

What is illusory thought? It is phenomena.
Illusory thought arises from the mind because of phenomena;
Mind abandons forms, that is "true suchness".

True suchness fills all space,
Because it fills all space,
True suchness is every Dharma,
Every Dharma is true suchness.

Abandon thoughts, cease thoughts, abandon forms,
Abandoning thoughts is ceasing thoughts,
Ceasing thoughts is true suchness,
True suchness is the suchness of non-duality,
Non-duality is without opposition or relativity.

Meditate, listen to the silence,
Let us abandon every illusory thought,
Abandoning illusion turn to truth, enter the form of the absolute truth.

True suchness is absolute truth,
Absolute truth is in every form.

十一面觀音矗立於靈鷲山最高點，護持十方法界眾生。

Eleven-faced Guanyin stands at the highest point of LJM,
looking after all the beings of the ten directions.

眞心如日

眞理是什麼？
眞理是普遍的、永恆的、不變的。
什麼是永恆性？
什麼是不變性？
什麼是普遍性？
在哪裡都可以找得到，
眞理無處不在，所以叫做普遍性。

眞理是一切萬有的核心，
實際上，也就是我們的眞心。
眞理就是我們的心，
我們的心就是眞理。

佛法就在探討眞理，
幫助我們把腦筋理順、把眞心顯現，
讓每個人的愛心凝聚一起，
受用這份永恆不變的本質、本性。

每個人有一顆眞心，
它像太陽一樣，可以覺照一切世間種種，
能夠明瞭眞假、事實。
只要你去覺照它，
就會發現到你的本質。

True Mind Like the Sun

What is the truth?
Truth is universal, eternal, unchanging.
What is eternal?
What is unchanging?
What is universal?
It can be found everywhere,
Truth fills the space, so it is called universal.

Truth is the core of every existing phenomena,
Actually it is our true mind.
Truth is our mind,
Our mind is the truth.

Dharma is the exploration of the truth,
It helps us smooth our mind, makes our true mind appear,
It brings together the love of everyone,
So we can all use this eternal, unchanging essential quality, our true nature.

Everybody has a true mind,
It is like the sun, it can illuminate all the things in the world,
It can understand what is true and false, what is fact.
Only if you illuminate the mind,
Will you discover your essential quality.

True Mind Like the Sun

What is the truth?
Truth is universal, eternal, unchanging.
What is eternal?
What is unchanging?
What is universal?
It can be found everywhere,
Truth fills the space, so it is called universal.

Truth is the core of every existing phenomena,
Actually it is our true mind.
Truth is our mind,
Our mind is the truth.

Dharma is the exploration of the truth,
It helps us smooth our mind, makes our true mind appear,
It brings together the love of everyone,
So we can all use this eternal, unchanging essential quality, our true nature.

Everybody has a true mind,
It is like the sun, it can illuminate all the things in the world,
It can understand what is true and false, what is fact.
Only if you illuminate the mind,
Will you discover your essential quality.

真理就是我們的心，我們的心就是真理。

Truth dwells in your own heart; your heart itself is truth.

清淨覺悟

修行即是證悟此心，
心是法界，心是生命，心即是解脫。
心即是佛，心也叫做眾生。

如何讓此心成佛？
心要成佛，要能覺悟，
覺悟要靠法，
法呢，唯有清淨，
從清淨來相應法，
從法來透視一切虛妄，
從透視一切虛妄，
證悟心的本來面目。

Pure Awakening

Dharma practice is to realize this mind,
Mind is the Dharma realm, mind is life, mind is liberation.
Mind is the Buddha, mind is also sentient beings.

How to make this mind become the Buddha?
If mind wants to become the Buddha, it has to awaken,
To awaken rely on the Dharma,
The Dharma of only purity,
Through purification become one with Dharma,
Through Dharma, see through all illusions,
From seeing through all illusions,
Realize the original face of your mind.

Pure Awakening

Dharma practice is to realize this mind,
Mind is the Dharma realm, mind is life, mind is liberation.
Mind is the Buddha, mind is also sentient beings.

How to make this mind become the Buddha?
If mind wants to become the Buddha, it has to awaken,
To awaken rely on the Dharma,
The Dharma of only purity.
Through purification become one with Dharma,
Through Dharma, see through all illusions,
From seeing through all illusions,
Realize the original face of your mind.

透視一切虛妄，證悟心的本來面目。

Seeing through all appearances,
you catch sight of your original nature.

明心見性

心是什麼？心長得什麼樣子？
心是圓的？方的？
什麼顏色？大小如何？
有頭？沒頭？有尾？沒尾？

對於心的參悟獲得徹底明瞭，
這就是明心。
對心的本質能夠了解，
這就是見性。
能夠明白心，知道心的本質，
就叫做明心見性。

心性也叫做法界性，
了解心性，就了解宇宙的一切。

Understanding the Mind, Seeing the True Nature

What is the mind? What does the mind look like?
Is it round or square?
What is the color? What is the size?
With a head? Without a head? With a tail? Without a tail?

Through contemplation and realization,obtain a thorough illumination of the mind,
This is understanding the mind.
Realizing the essential nature of the mind,
This is seeing the true nature.
Illuminating the mind, directly knowing the essential nature,
This is called understanding the mind and seeing the true nature.

The nature of the mind is also the nature of the Dharma realm,
Understanding the nature of the mind,
Is understanding everything in the universe.

Understanding the Mind, Seeing the True Nature

What is the mind? What does the mind look like?
Is it round or square?
What is the color? What is the size?
With a head? Without a head? With a tail? Without a tail?

Through contemplation and realization, obtain a thorough illumination of the mind,
This is understanding the mind.
Realizing the essential nature of the mind,
This is seeing the true nature.
Illuminating the mind, directly knowing the essential nature,
This is called understanding the mind and seeing the true nature.

The nature of the mind is also the nature of the Dharma realm,
Understanding the nature of the mind,
Is understanding everything in the universe.

明心見性，了解宇宙的一切。

Illuminating your self-nature,
Understanding everything in the universe.

法界一心

這個世界可以分割嗎？
是沒有辦法分割的，
所以一心就是法界，
法界就是一心。
就從這個角度，去理解離苦得樂的方法。

痛苦，是緣於我們的迷惑，
是因為我們的分別心。
分別心造成了你我的分別，
造成相對、對立的生命；
因為對立，所以爭執、不和諧。
因為對立，所以獲得一個困擾的生命。

真理是絕對的，沒有相對，
每一個人就是我，我就是每一個人；
一切即是我，我即是一切。

在這當中，
沒有相對的生命呈現，
是絕對的生命，共同的生命體。

Dharma Realm, One Mind

Can this world be divided up into pieces?
No, it can't be divided up,
Therefore one mind is the Dharma realm,
The Dharma realm is one mind.
From this point of view, comprehend the method of abandoning
suffering and achieving happiness.

Suffering, is caused by our delusion,
Because of our discriminating mind.
Discriminating mind creates the distinction between you and I,
It creates life that is relative and in opposition to others;
Because there is opposition, there is argument and disharmony.
Because there is opposition, a life of affliction comes about.

Truth is absolute, it is not relative,
Every person is I, I am every person;
All is I, I is all.

In this truth,
There is no manifestation of relative life,
There is only the absolute life, one community of life.

Dharma Realm, One Mind

Can this world be divided up into pieces?
No, it can't be divided up,
Therefore one mind is the Dharma realm,
The Dharma realm is one mind.
From this point of view, comprehend the method of abandoning
suffering and achieving happiness.

Suffering, is caused by our delusion,
Because of our discriminating mind.
Discriminating mind creates the distinction between you and I,
It creates life that is relative and in opposition to others;
Because there is opposition, there is argument and disharmony,
Because there is opposition, a life of affliction comes about.

Truth is absolute, it is not relative,
Every person is I, I am every person;
All is I, I is all.

In this truth,
There is no manifestation of relative life,
There is only the absolute life, one community of life.

奉行觀音行願，矢志度眾。

Emulating the great compassion of Guanyin.

行願之人

A Person with a Vow to Action

這人，
This person,

名慈悲。
Named compassion.

是菩薩的化現，
Is the manifestation of the Bodhisattva,

是覺悟的燈塔。
Is the lighthouse of awakening.

自性懺悔

我要向誰懺悔呢？
是請佛傾聽我的懺悔啊！

眾生原本就是佛！
每一個人最根本的源頭就是佛！
懺悔，就是對自己內在的源頭——「自性佛」來懺悔的。
這個最本初的佛性，佛與一切眾生是一樣的，
它就在我們裡面。

但是我們迷失了，
我們塗了很多的粉——骯髒的粉、快樂的粉、各種的粉，
這些粉末模糊了我們的生命全體，
使我們不認識自己的本來面目：
只看到自己的骯髒，
而看不到自性佛的莊嚴。

我們今天用懺悔法門來拔除這些不乾淨的垢染，
慢慢越洗越乾淨，
通通洗乾淨以後，
到最後就會看到我們本來的佛。

Repentance to the Self Nature

To whom should I repent?
It is to request the Buddha to listen to my repentance!

Sentient beings are originally Buddhas!
Every person's most essential origin is Buddha!
Repentance is to repent to one's inner origin - "Buddha of Self-nature".
This most primary Buddha nature in Buddha,
And all sentient beings is the same,
It is within ourselves.

But we are lost,
We put on a lot of make-up –
Dirty make-up, happy make-up, every kind of make-up,
These kinds of make-up obscure the unity of our whole life,
And make us unable to recognize our original face;
We can only see our defilements,
And we can't see the solemnity of the Buddha of Self-nature.

Today we use the repentance method to uproot the dirty defilements,
The more you repent, gradually the more you become purified,
After the complete purification,
Finally we can see our original Buddha.

Repentance to the Self Nature

To whom should I repent?
It is to request the Buddha to listen to my repentance!

Sentient beings are originally Buddhas!
Every person's most essential origin is Buddha!
Repentance is to repent to one's inner origin - "Buddha of Self-nature".
This most primary Buddha nature in Buddha,
And all sentient beings is the same,
It is within ourselves.

But we are lost,
We put on a lot of make-up –
Dirty make-up, happy make-up, every kind of make-up,
These kinds of make-up obscure the unity of our whole life,
And make us unable to recognize our original face;
We can only see our defilements,
And we can't see the solemnity of the Buddha of Self-nature.

Today we use the repentance method to uproot the dirty defilements,
The more you repent, gradually the more you become purified,
After the complete purification,
Finally we can see our original Buddha.

凝聚慈悲善念，迴向地球平安。

Accumulating merit and dedicating it to world peace.

大慈悲心

找到眞心，可以怎麼樣呢？
傳承覺悟，傳承人與人之間的關係。

在宇宙中一切眾生和我的關係是什麼？
當發現眞理時，
會看到宇宙一切眾生和我是「生命共同體」，
他們是我，我是他們，
彼此是無法分割的生命體。

所以對萬有、萬事、萬物，
都要有一份悲憫心、慈悲心。
對一切慈悲，
一切才會對你慈悲。

對生命共同體的一切眾生，生起奉獻服務的心，
這宇宙的一切眾生，才會爲你奉獻服務。

Great Compassion Mind

Find the true mind, what can it do?
Pass down awakening, pass down the relationships between people.

What is the relationship between every sentient being and me in the universe?
When the truth is discovered,
One can see that every sentient being in the universe and me are "One Body of life",
They are I, I am them,
The One Body can never be divided.

Towards all existing phenomena, matters and things,
We should have sympathy and compassion.
Be compassionate to everything,
Everything will be compassionate towards you.

Give rise to a mind of dedication and service toward every sentient being in the One
Body of life,
Then all the sentient beings in the universe will dedicate themselves to serving you.

Great Compassion Mind

Find the true mind, what can it do?
Pass down awakening, pass down the relationships between people.

What is the relationship between every sentient being and me in the universe?
When the truth is discovered,
One can see that every sentient being in the universe and me are "One Body of life",
They are I, I am them,
The One Body can never be divided.

Towards all existing phenomena, matters and things,
We should have sympathy and compassion.
Be compassionate to everything,
Everything will be compassionate towards you.

Give rise to a mind of dedication and service toward every sentient being in the One
Body of life,
Then all the sentient beings in the universe will dedicate themselves to serving you.

對宇宙一切眾生，生起服務奉獻的本心。

The basic intention to serve and benefit all sentient beings.

分享證悟

菩薩叫做「菩提薩埵」，就是覺有情，
是自覺、覺他的意思。

自覺，就是把自己修好，
真正受用自己修行的成果。

菩薩道就是把自己修行的成果，
布施給還沒有得到的、還沒有享用到的眾生，
讓一切眾生獲得自己所證悟的法喜。

一者是自利，一者是利他，
修行是自利、攝心；
菩薩道是慈、悲、喜、捨的，
這兩者是無法分開的。

如果沒有自受用的經驗，
如何能夠分享給眾生這受用的經驗呢？
所以「修行」是證明佛法，
「菩薩道」是把自己所證的境界分享給眾生，
大家一同享用佛法。

Sharing Awakening

Bodhisattva means awakened sentient beings,
Awakening yourself and awakening others.

Awakening yourself, attain self realization through practice,
And truly use the results of self practice.

The Bodhisattva path is to use the result of self practice,
Offering the result to sentient beings who are not yet awakened and not able
to use their own result,
Let every sentient being share the Dharma joy of the Bodhisattva's awakening.
One aspect benefits one self, the other aspect benefit others,
Dharma practice is to benefit one self, focus the mind;
Bodhisattva path is love, compassion, joy and equanimity,
These two aspects cannot be separated.

If one doesn't have the experience of using the result,
How can one share the experience of using the result with sentient beings?
So Dharma practice is to prove Buddha Dharma,
The Bodhisattva path is to share with sentient beings the stages that one has
realized,
Everybody enjoys and uses the Dharma.

Sharing Awakening

Bodhisattva means awakened sentient beings,
Awakening yourself and awakening others.

Awakening yourself, attain self realization through practice,
And truly use the results of self practice.

The Bodhisattva path is to use the result of self practice,
Offering the result to sentient beings who are not yet awakened and not able
to use their own result.
Let every sentient being share the Dharma joy of the Bodhisattva's awakening.
One aspect benefits one self, the other aspect benefit others,
Dharma practice is to benefit one self, focus the mind;
Bodhisattva path is love, compassion, joy and equanimity,
These two aspects cannot be separated.

If one doesn't have the experience of using the result,
How can one share the experience of using the result with sentient beings?
So Dharma practice is to prove Buddha Dharma,
The Bodhisattva path is to share with sentient beings the stages that one has
realized,
Everybody enjoys and uses the Dharma.

以慈悲喜捨四無量心，行菩薩道。

Making the Four Divine Abidings—compassion,
loving kindness, sympathetic joy, and equanimity—the basis of the Bodhisattva practice.

靈覺生活

為什麼要修行呢？
是為了要改變業力、習氣。

我們要變化氣質，
讓身心超越執著與煩惱，
然後轉化日常生活中的慣性與生活習慣。

是不是修行人就沒有生活了？
修行人也是有生活的。
在生活當中，毫不含糊、清清楚楚，
在寂靜的靈覺裡面，明明白白地去生活；
而不是迷執煩惱，累積垢染，
造成很多的迷惑，
在未來的生命裡面，產生業力的糾纏，
而帶來彼此的痛苦。

把心收攝，管得住自己，
才能夠去利益眾生；
管不住自己，依舊和習氣環扣，
結果還是業力輪迴。

讓真心長住、善業永續，
這是我們修行的目的。

Awakened Spiritual Life

Why practice Dharma?
To change one's karma, one's habitual tendencies.

We need to change our disposition,
To make the body and mind go beyond attachments and afflictions,
Transform the tendencies and habits of every day life.

Doesn't the Dharma practitioner have no life?
The Dharma practitioner also has a life.
In the life, nothing is blurred, everything is clear,
In the tranquility of awakened spirituality, lead a luminous life;
If one is not detached from affliction and accumulating defilements,
One will create a lot of delusion,
The future life produces the entanglements of karma,
And brings suffering to each other.

Only if one focuses the mind and control one's self,
One can benefit sentient beings;
If one cannot control one's self, one will still connect to habitual tendencies,
The result is still karmic reincarnation.

Maintain the longevity of the true mind, sustain wholesome karma,
This is the purpose of Dharma practice.

Awakened Spiritual Life

Why practice Dharma?
To change one's karma, one's habitual tendencies.

We need to change our disposition,
To make the body and mind go beyond attachments and afflictions,
Transform the tendencies and habits of every day life.

Doesn't the Dharma practitioner have no life?
The Dharma practitioner also has a life.
In the life, nothing is blurred, everything is clear.
In the tranquility of awakened spirituality, lead a luminous life;
If one is not detached from affliction and accumulating defilements,
One will create a lot of delusion,
The future life produces the entanglements of karma,
And brings suffering to each other.

Only if one focuses the mind and control one's self,
One can benefit sentient beings;
If one cannot control one's self, one will still connect to habitual tendencies,
The result is still karmic reincarnation.

Maintain the longevity of the true mind, sustain wholesome karma,
This is the purpose of Dharma practice.

真心長住，清清楚楚、明明白白地生活。

Abiding in the true mind and cultivating clarity and understanding.

空中妙有

佛法就是究竟利他，
能究竟利他，就能得到大樂。

大樂又叫做空樂，
不能究竟利他，即使證空也不樂。
要享有空的快樂，就要究竟利他。

利他的工作就是能夠妙有。
什麼是「妙有」呢？
本來空就很妙了，為什麼還要妙有呢？

妙有始於慈悲，
能覺醒一切，
能使一切眾生產生覺醒跟愛心。

覺醒跟愛心是一體的，
缺了其中之一，就不能成佛。
佛是悲智雙運，空有雙運。
雙運就是一種體性的變化。

Wonderful Existence in Emptiness

Buddha Dharma is absolutely altruistic,
If one can be absolutely altruistic, one can achieve great happiness.

Great happiness is also called the happiness of emptiness,
If one cannot be absolutely altruistic,
Even realizing emptiness one cannot be happy.
If one wants to enjoy the happiness of emptiness,
one must be absolutely altruistic.

Altruistic work is to have a wonderful existence.
What is "wonderful existence"?
Emptiness was originally wonderful,
why should there be wonderful existence?

Wonderful existence arises from compassion,
It can awaken everything,
It can make every sentient being generate awakening and loving-kindness.

Awakening and loving-kindness are unified,
If one is absent, one cannot become a Buddha.
The Buddha is the dual method of compassion and wisdom,
emptiness and existence,
The dual method is a kind of transformation of our true nature.

Wonderful Existence in Emptiness

Buddha Dharma is absolutely altruistic,
If one can be absolutely altruistic, one can achieve great happiness.

Great happiness is also called the happiness of emptiness,
If one cannot be absolutely altruistic,
Even realizing emptiness one cannot be happy.
If one wants to enjoy the happiness of emptiness,
one must be absolutely altruistic.

Altruistic work is to have a wonderful existence.
What is "wonderful existence"?
Emptiness was originally wonderful,
why should there be wonderful existence?

Wonderful existence arises from compassion,
It can awaken everything,
It can make every sentient being generate awakening and loving-kindness.

Awakening and loving-kindness are unified,
If one is absent, one cannot become a Buddha.
The Buddha is the dual method of compassion and wisdom,
emptiness and existence,
The dual method is a kind of transformation of our true nature.

究竟利他，覺醒一切眾生。

Benefitting and enlightening others.

成就淨土

成佛從發菩提心開始，
生生世世必須自覺覺他、自利利他，
不管身為何種生命型態，
都要一直地、不斷地、持續地做，
便會成就非常多的善緣。

善緣會形成善業，好比是軟體；
善業再形成硬體，諸如星球與星系。
這些都不是無中生有的，
而是相互環扣、互為因果。

每一個人只要發心成佛，
然後不斷地做善事和成就覺悟，
將來就會擁有廣大的報土，
每一個佛國都是這樣來的，
這就是佛法的核心思想，
也是宇宙的核心力量。

Perfection of the Pure Land

Becoming a Buddha starts from generating bodhicitta,
Life after life one must awaken oneself and others,
Benefit oneself and others,
No matter what form of life one is born as,
One must always continuously,
Constantly awaken and benefit oneself and others,
Then one will achieve enormous virtuous karmic cause.

Virtuous karmic cause is like the software;
Then this becomes the virtuous karma, which is like the hardware,
It is also like planets forming a galaxy.
All of these have not emerged from nothingness,
They are all interconnected, interdependent on cause and effect.

Only if a person is determined to become Buddha,
And continuously does virtuous deeds and realizes awakening,
One will then own an enormous territory as a result,
This is how every Buddha World came to be,
This is the core concept of Buddha Dharma,
And the core energy of the universe.

Perfection of the Pure Land

Becoming a Buddha starts from generating bodhicitta,
Life after life one must awaken oneself and others,
Benefit oneself and others,
No matter what form of life one is born as,
One must always continuously,
Constantly awaken and benefit oneself and others,
Then one will achieve enormous virtuous karmic cause.

Virtuous karmic cause is like the software;
Then this becomes the virtuous karma, which is like the hardware,
It is also like planets forming a galaxy.
All of these have not emerged from nothingness,
They are all interconnected, interdependent on cause and effect.

Only if a person is determined to become Buddha,
And continuously does virtuous deeds and realizes awakening,
One will then own an enormous territory as a result,
This is how every Buddha World came to be,
This is the core concept of Buddha Dharma,
And the core energy of the universe.

發菩提心，自覺覺他，成就莊嚴佛土。

Generating *bodhicitta*, enlightening oneself and others,
and creating a wonderful Buddha-land.

常隨佛轉

只要離開佛法，
福氣就會愈來愈小，
因為一離開善緣、善業的架構，
你就失去了環扣佛法的力量。
變成一個人轉，
而不是和佛法一起轉。

當我們和佛法一起轉，
環扣著宇宙中覺悟、慈悲的力量，
環扣著自覺覺他、自利利他的力量，
因而和佛法的大磁場、大能量環扣一起，
就會所求如願。

為什麼老是覺得不如意呢？
因為我們沒有環扣住佛法的力量，
離開了佛法的軌道，
所以就不在善緣、善業的大循環裡面，
而開始自己的小循環，
這當然沒有福氣啦！

如果想要福氣無盡，
一定要發菩提心直至成佛。

Always Follow the Buddha and Revolve in the Dharma

If one leaves the Buddha Dharma,
One's fortune will become smaller and smaller,
Because one has left the structure of the virtuous causes and virtuous karma,
One has lost the power to connect with the Dharma,
Come to be revolving only around oneself,
Instead of revolving together with Buddha Dharma.

When we revolve together with Buddha Dharma
We are connecting with the universal power of awakening and compassion,
Connecting with the power of awakening and benefiting oneself and others,
Because of the connection to the great magnetic field and the great energy of Dharma,
All our wishes will be fulfilled.

Why do we always feel things are not the way we want?
Because we don't have the connection to the power of the Buddha Dharma,
Leaving the orbit of the Buddha Dharma,
We are not in the great circle of virtuous causes and virtuous karma,
We start our own small circle,
But of course this doesn't create good fortune!

If we want to have endless good fortune,
We must develop bodhicitta until we become Buddha.

Always Follow the Buddha and Revolve in the Dharma

If one leaves the Buddha Dharma,
One's fortune will become smaller and smaller,
Because one has left the structure of the virtuous causes and virtuous karma,
One has lost the power to connect with the Dharma,
Come to be revolving only around oneself,
Instead of revolving together with Buddha Dharma.

When we revolve together with Buddha Dharma
We are connecting with the universal power of awakening and compassion,
Connecting with the power of awakening and benefiting oneself and others,
Because of the connection to the great magnetic field and the great energy of Dharma,
All our wishes will be fulfilled.

Why do we always feel things are not the way we want?
Because we don't have the connection to the power of the Buddha Dharma,
Leaving the orbit of the Buddha Dharma,
We are not in the great circle of virtuous causes and virtuous karma,
We start our own small circle,
But of course this doesn't create good fortune!

If we want to have endless good fortune,
We must develop bodhicitta until we become Buddha.

環扣覺悟慈悲的力量，直至成佛。

Cultivating the wisdom and compassion which culminate in Buddhahood.

三身起用

佛陀成就三身——法、報、化三身。

「法身」就是不死的靈性，
是生命共同體，
也是整體的宇宙。

「報身」就是無礙的智慧，
每一個人的自心本性都是光明的，
就像一盞明亮的燈。

「化身」就是無量的慈悲，
當每一個人都生起慈悲心，
這就是佛的化身。

靈鷲山所推動的正是從「慈悲」開始，
做到「覺明」再到「同體大悲」，
這就是「法、報、化三身同時起用」，
也成就了華嚴世界。

The Application of the Three Bodies

Buddha attained three bodies - Dharmakaya, Sambhogakaya, Nirmanakaya.

"Dharmakaya" is the undying spiritual nature,
the community of life in One Body,
the entire body of the universe.

"Sambhogakaya" is the wisdom with no obstacles,
Everyone's original nature of mind is radiant,
Like a brilliant light.

"Nirmanakaya" is unmeasurable compassion,
When everyone's compassion arises,
This is the manifestation of the Buddha.

What Ling Jiou Mountain is promoting starts with "compassion",
To "luminous awareness", then to "compassion with equanimity",
This is the simultaneous application of the "three bodies of the Buddha",
To achieve the Avatamsaka World.

The Application of the Three Bodies

Buddha attained three bodies - Dharmakaya, Sambhogakaya, Nirmanakaya.

"Dharmakaya" is the undying spiritual nature,
the community of life in One Body,
the entire body of the universe.

"Sambhogakaya" is the wisdom with no obstacles,
Everyone's original nature of mind is radiant,
Like a brilliant light.

"Nirmanakaya" is unmeasurable compassion,
When everyone's compassion arises,
This is the manifestation of the Buddha.

What Ling Jiou Mountain is promoting starts with "compassion",
To "luminous awareness", then to "compassion with equanimity",
This is the simultaneous application of the "three bodies of the Buddha",
To achieve the Avatamsaka World.

法、報、化三身起用，成就華嚴世界。

Utilizing the *Dharmakaya*, *Sambhogakaya*, and *Nirmanakaya* to create the Huayan realm.

地藏與我

有一次我帶了很多人，
去中國九華山朝拜地藏菩薩；
到了地藏洞裡面，
感覺很有靈氣，
就坐下來誦持地藏菩薩的名號，

之後不禁思考著：
到底我是地藏菩薩？
還是地藏菩薩是我？

雖然我和地藏菩薩由於因緣不同，
所以外在形狀不同，
可是覺得內在都是一樣的。

五濁惡世中，
人生苦難就像地獄一樣，
如果我們能夠腳踏地藏菩薩的願力，
去學習佛法、實踐佛法、度化眾生，
那麼我和地藏菩薩的內在又有什麼不同呢？

Ksitigarbha and I

Once I took many people,
To Jiu Hua Mountain in China to prostrate to Ksitigarbha Bodhisattva,
In the Ksitigarbha Cave,
There was a very spiritual feeling,
We just sat down and recited the name of Ksitigarbha Bodhisattva,

After that I can't help contemplating:
In the end, am I Ksitigarbha Bodhisattva?
Or is Ksitigarbha Bodhisattva me?

Even though the conditions of Ksitigarbha Bodhisattva and me are different,
The external form is not the same,
But I felt the inner nature is all the same.

In the evil period of five turbidities,
The suffering in life is hell-like,
If we can follow in the steps of Ksitigarbha Bodhisattva's vows,
Learn the Buddha Dharma, practice the Buddha Dharma,
Enlighten sentient beings,
Then what is the difference between the inner nature of Ksitigarbha
Bodhisattva and me?

Ksitigarbha and I

Once I took many people,
To Jiu Hua Mountain in China to prostrate to Ksitigarbha Bodhisattva,
In the Ksitigarbha Cave,
There was a very spiritual feeling,
We just sat down and recited the name of Ksitigarbha Bodhisattva,

After that I can't help contemplating:
In the end, am I Ksitigarbha Bodhisattva?
Or is Ksitigarbha Bodhisattva me?

Even though the conditions of Ksitigarbha Bodhisattva and me are different,
The external form is not the same,
But I felt the inner nature is all the same.

In the evil period of five turbidities,
The suffering in life is hell-like,
If we can follow in the steps of Ksitigarbha Bodhisattva's vows,
Learn the Buddha Dharma, practice the Buddha Dharma,
Enlighten sentient beings,
Then what is the difference between the inner nature of Ksitigarbha
Bodhisattva and me?

地藏道場中央的「大願舍利塔」，
象徵地藏菩薩「地獄不空，誓不成佛。」的堅定道心。

The Great Vow Stupa at the center of the Dizang Mandala represents Dizang Bodhisattva's
vow to delay the attainment of Buddhahood until all the hell realms are emptied.

頂戴佛陀

我十分感恩釋迦佛，
讓我有機會學習佛法。

如果沒有佛，
我也就沒有佛法可學，
內心就快樂不起來，
對於生、老、病、死一點辦法也沒有。

今天我知道如何解脫生、老、病、死，
知道人生怎麼做，才能得到最大的福氣，
怎麼樣做，才能得到最大智慧，
因為我已經掌握了生命的方向盤，
得到這麼大的收穫與快樂，
都是釋迦佛給予的。

要如何報答釋迦佛呢？
只有一個方法：承先啟後。

只有把佛的法傳承下去，
用祂的那份苦心來傳承法，
把佛法傳給每一個人，
使大家都能夠解脫、都能夠快樂，
這就是頂戴釋迦佛的使命。

Putting Buddha on Your Head

I am deeply grateful to Shakyamuni Buddha,
For giving me the opportunity to learn the Dharma.

If there was no Buddha,
I wouldn't have any Buddha Dharma to learn,
There wouldn't be any happiness in my heart,
There would be no way to cope with birth, old age, sickness and death.

Today I know how to be liberated from birth, old age, sickness and death,
Knowing what to do in life to gain the greatest fortune,
What to do to achieve the greatest wisdom,
Because I have already mastered the steering wheel of life,
Attaining such great harvest and happiness,
All this comes from Shakyamuni Buddha.

How to repay Shakyamuni Buddha?
There is only one way:
To continue the lineage and enlighten the next generation.

To pass down the teachings,
To take the same troubles as Shakyamuni Buddha to spread the Dharma,
To transmit the Dharma to everyone,
To make everybody liberated and happy,
This is the mission of putting Shakyamuni Buddha on your head.

Putting Buddha on Your Head

I am deeply grateful to Shakyamuni Buddha,
For giving me the opportunity to learn the Dharma.

If there was no Buddha,
I wouldn't have any Buddha Dharma to learn,
There wouldn't be any happiness in my heart,
There would be no way to cope with birth, old age, sickness and death.

Today I know how to be liberated from birth, old age, sickness and death,
Knowing what to do in life to gain the greatest fortune,
What to do to achieve the greatest wisdom,
Because I have already mastered the steering wheel of life,
Attaining such great harvest and happiness,
All this comes from Shakyamuni Buddha.

How to repay Shakyamuni Buddha?
There is only one way:
To continue the lineage and enlighten the next generation.

To pass down the teachings,
To take the same troubles as Shakyamuni Buddha to spread the Dharma,
To transmit the Dharma to everyone,
To make everybody liberated and happy,
This is the mission of putting Shakyamuni Buddha on your head.

傳承佛法，頂戴釋迦佛使命。

Reverently propagating the Buddhadharma.

國家圖書館出版品預行編目 (CIP) 資料

山海天人：心遊法界 / 釋心道著.
-- 二版. --
新北市：靈鷲山般若出版, 2015.08
面；　公分
ISBN 978-986-6324-90-1(平裝)
1.佛教說法 225.4　　104014276

山海天人　心遊法界

Mountain, Ocean, Sky and People :
A Mind Journey through the Dharma Realm

作　　者：釋心道
總 策 劃：釋了意
主　　編：洪淑妍
責　　編：汪姿郡
美　　編：黃偉哲
英文審校：Dr. Maria Reis Habito

Author : Dharma Master Hsin Tao
General Planer : Ven. Liao Yi Shih
Editor in Chief : Hung, Shu-yen
Editor in charge : Wang, Zi-jun
Art Editor : Huang, Wei-jer
English Proofreading : Dr. Maria Reis Habito

發 行 人：歐陽慕親
出版發行：財團法人靈鷲山般若文教基金會附設出版社
地　　址：23444新北市永和區保生路2號21樓
電　　話：02-2232-1008
傳　　眞：02-2232-1010
網　　址：www.093books.com.tw
讀者信箱：books@ljm.org.tw
總 經 銷：飛鴻國際行銷股份有限公司
法律顧問：永然聯合法律事務所
印　　刷：皇城廣告印刷事業股份有限公司
劃撥帳戶：財團法人靈鷲山般若文教基金會附設出版社
劃撥帳號：18887793
二版一刷：二〇一五年八月
定　　價：550元
I S B N：978-986-6324-90-1

Publisher : Ouyang, Mu-qin
Published by and The postal service is allocated :
Ling Jiou Mountain Press, Ling Jiou Mountain Prajna Cultural
and Educational Foundation
Address : 21F., No.2, Baosheng Rd., Yonghe Dist.,
New Taipei City 23444, Taiwan (R.O.C)
Tel : (02)-2232-1008
Fax : (02)-2232-1010
Website : www.093books.com.tw
E-mail : books@ljm.org.tw
Distributor : Flying Horn International Marketing Co., Ltd.
Legal Consultant : Y. R. Lee & Partners Attorneys at Law
Printing : Huang Cheng Printing Company, Ltd.
Account number :18887793
The First Printing of the Second Edition : August, 2015
List Price : NT$550
ISBN : 978-986-6324-90-1

靈鷲山般若書坊